FAMOUS ARTISTS

MICHELANGELO

JEN GREEN

BARRON'S

CONTENTS

The Creation of Eve, from the ceiling of the Sistine Chapel

FAMOUS ARTISTS
MICHELANGELO

The author, Jen Green, is an editor and author of several art books for children.

Designer   Peter Bennett
Picture research Emma Krikler
Illustrators   Michaela Stewart
                  Peter Bennett

First edition for the United States, Canada, and the Philippines
published 1994 by Barron's Educational Series, Inc.

Designed and produced by
Aladdin Books Ltd
28 Percy Street
London W1P 9FF

First published in
Great Britain in 1993 by
Watts Books
96 Leonard Street
London EC2A 4RH

All inquiries should be addressed to:
Barron's Educational Series, Inc.
250 Wireless Boulevard
Hauppauge, New York 11788

Library of Congress Catalog Card No.: 94-14292

Green, Jen.
Michelangelo / Jen Green
p. cm. – (Famous artists)
"First published in Great Britain in 1993 by Watts Books"–T.p. verso
Includes index.
ISBN 0-8120-6461-5 (hardcover). –ISBN 0-8120-1998-9 (pbk.)
1. Michelangelo Buonarroti, 1475-1564. 2. Artists–Italy–Biography. I. Title. II. Series.
N6923.B9G74   1994
709'.2–dc20
[B]   94-14292
CIP

International Standard Book No. 0-8120-6461-5 (hardcover)
                                0-8120-1998-9 (paperback)

Printed in Belgium
4567 4208 987654321

INTRODUCTION

Michelangelo Buonarroti was born near Florence in 1475 and died in Rome in 1564. He spent his long life creating works of great beauty, and when he died at the age of 89 he was already acknowledged as one of the greatest artists of his time. The frescoes he painted in the Sistine Chapel and his carvings, such as David, are considered among the finest art treasures of the world. He was one of the first artists to be seen as a genius rather than a mere craftsman commanded by patrons.

This book explores Michelangelo's development from apprentice to master, and describes how his major works came to be created. Below you can see how the book is organized. Text and captions help to explain the history of Michelangelo's works, but your own reactions are important too. As you look at the paintings and sculptures in this book, ask yourself what you think the artist wanted to achieve and be aware of your own feelings about his work.

About the artist's work at the time

The story of the artist's life

Illustration of the artist's home or environment

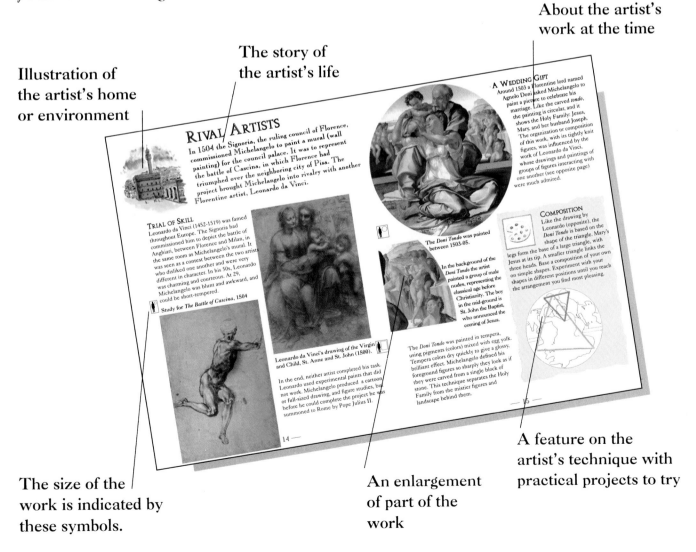

RIVAL ARTISTS
In 1504 the Signoria, the ruling council of Florence, commissioned Michelangelo to paint a mural (wall painting) for the council palace. It was to represent the battle of Cascina, in which Florence had triumphed over the neighboring city of Pisa. The project brought Michelangelo into rivalry with another Florentine artist, Leonardo da Vinci.

TRIAL OF SKILL
Leonardo da Vinci (1452-1519) was famed throughout Europe. The Signoria had commissioned him to depict the battle of Anghiari, between Florence and Milan, in the same room as Michelangelo's mural. It was seen as a contest between the two artists who disliked one another and were very different in character. In his 50s, Leonardo was charming and courteous. At 29, Michelangelo was blunt and awkward, and could be short-tempered.

Study for The Battle of Cascina, 1504

Leonardo da Vinci's drawing of the Virgin and Child, St. Anne and St. John (1500).

In the end, neither artist completed his task. Leonardo used experimental paints that did not work. Michelangelo produced a cartoon, or full-sized drawing, and figure studies, but before he could complete the project he was summoned to Rome by Pope Julius II.

A WEDDING GIFT
Around 1503 a Florentine lord named Agnolo Doni asked Michelangelo to paint a picture to celebrate his marriage. Like the carved tondo, the painting is circular, and it shows the Holy Family: Jesus, Mary, and her husband Joseph. The organization or composition of this work, with its tightly knit figures, was influenced by the work of Leonardo da Vinci, whose drawings and paintings of groups of figures interacting with one another (see opposite page) were much admired.

The Doni Tondo was painted between 1503-05.

In the background of the Doni Tondo the artist painted a group of male nudes, representing the classical age before Christianity. The boy in the mid-ground is St. John the Baptist, who announced the coming of Jesus.

The Doni Tondo was painted in tempera, using pigments (colors) mixed with egg yolk. Tempera colors dry quickly to give a glossy, brilliant effect. Michelangelo defined his foreground figures so sharply they look as if they were carved from a single block of stone. This technique separates the Holy Family from the mistier figures and landscape behind them.

COMPOSITION
Like the drawing by Leonardo (opposite), the Doni Tondo is based on the shape of the triangle. Mary's legs form the base of a large triangle, with Jesus at its tip. A smaller triangle links the three heads. Base a composition of your own on simple shapes. Experiment with your shapes in different positions until you reach the arrangement you find most pleasing.

A feature on the artist's technique with practical projects to try

The size of the work is indicated by these symbols.

An enlargement of part of the work

EARLY LIFE

Michelangelo was born near the end of a great period in art history called the Renaissance. Since 1300 the rediscovery of the arts of ancient Greece and Rome had caused painting and sculpture to flourish in Italy. The cities of northern Italy, especially Florence, near Michelangelo's birth-place, had become centers of art and learning.

Michelangelo Buonarroti was born on March 6, 1475, in Caprese (above), a village in the hills of Tuscany in central Italy. His family was aristocratic, but had fallen on hard times. Michelangelo's mother was unable to breast-feed him, so he was sent to a wet nurse nearby. His nurse's husband was a stone cutter, and Michelangelo later used to joke that he had gained his skill with hammer and chisel from his nurse's milk.

The Battle of the Centaurs, 1491-92

APPRENTICESHIP

Michelangelo's mother died when he was six. From the age of ten he attended school in Florence and showed the most interest in drawing. By 13 he had decided that he wanted to be an artist. At first his father opposed this and beat him. But in 1488 he was allowed to become an apprentice of Domenico Ghirlandaio, one of the leading painters in Florence. In Ghirlandaio's workshop Michelangelo learned about drawing and fresco painting (see page 19).

Michelangelo sketched this figure from *The Tribute Money* by Masaccio (shown opposite) at 14.

EARLY WORKS

In Lorenzo's palace Michelangelo made the two remarkable carvings shown here. Both are examples of *relief* sculpture, carved into a flat surface of stone and designed to be seen from the front only. *The Madonna of the Stairs*, an example of low relief, is carved into a slab of marble less than two inches (5 cm) thick. It shows the Christian figures of the Virgin Mary with her child, Jesus. *The Battle of the Centaurs* is carved in much higher relief. It shows a scene from Greek legend, a fight between men and Centaurs, mythical creatures that were half human, half horse. The carving is full of movement.

The Madonna of the Stairs, 1491-92

COPYING ARTISTS

There is a great deal that can be learned from the great masters. In Florence Michelangelo sketched the wall paintings by Giotto and Masaccio (below) and admired the statues by Donatello and Verrocchio that stood in the squares. Visit local museums and art galleries yourself, and study and copy the works you like best.

IN THE MEDICI PALACE

At this time the republic of Florence was controlled by the wealthy Medici family. Its head was Lorenzo "the Magnificent," a great patron of the arts. Renaissance patrons and artists saw their age as a rebirth of classical civilization. In 1489 Michelangelo was invited to study classical sculpture in Lorenzo's palace under Bertoldo de Giovanni, who had been a pupil of the great sculptor Donatello. Michelangelo's carving so impressed Lorenzo that he took the boy into his own household. He was given a purple cloak to wear and was educated with Lorenzo's own son, Giovanni, and his nephew, Giulio.

In Search of a Patron

In 1492 Lorenzo the Magnificent died, and Michelangelo's carefree time as guest in the Medici Palace was over. Florence entered a time of trouble, and Michelangelo was forced to seek patronage elsewhere. His search took him to Bologna and then to Rome, where he produced his first major works.

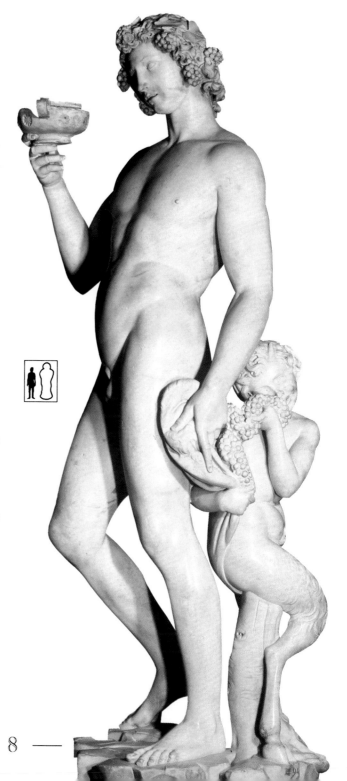

The Traveling Sculptor

In 1494 French armies invaded northern Italy. The Medici were expelled from Florence. Michelangelo went to Bologna, where he carved three small statues for the great tomb of St. Dominic. In 1496, in search of work, he traveled to Rome. At the time, an artist's subject was decided by the patron who paid for the commission. Wealthy churchmen would choose a biblical subject, while a prince or merchant might choose a scene from classical mythology. In Rome a rich banker named Jacopo Galli asked him for a marble statue of Bacchus, the Roman god of wine.

Bacchus was sculpted between 1496-97, when the artist was 21.

Unlike the relief carvings Michelangelo produced in 1491-92, Bacchus was a "carving in the round," designed to be seen from all sides. The sculptor portrayed Bacchus as a young man too drunk to notice that his grapes were being nibbled by the little goat-legged satyr behind him.

STATUE OF SORROW

In 1498 Michelangelo was engaged by a French cardinal, Jean Villiers, to produce a marble pietà for his tomb. The word *pietà* means "pity" in Italian. In art a pietà is an image of the Virgin Mary cradling her dead son Jesus. The theme was common in northern Europe, but unusual in Italy.

Previous versions were often awkward and ungainly, but Michelangelo's sculpture was graceful and lifelike. The artist made every detail perfect. Notice how the weight of Jesus's arm supported by Mary has made the skin bulge under his shoulder. Michelangelo took great care in carving the elaborate folds of the garments and giving his work a high polish. Those who came to view the sculpture marveled at its beauty and were moved by the sorrow shown on Mary's face. They were astonished that such a magnificent sculpture had been made by an artist of 24. Today, hundreds of years later, this work still has power to move us.

Pietà, 1498-1500. Mary's sash bears the artist's name; this was the only time he signed a work.

THE STATES OF ITALY

In Michelangelo's day the unified country of Italy did not exist. The peninsula was made up of about 14 separate states, controlled by cities such as Florence, Milan, and Venice. The pope ruled the Papal States, a large territory in central Italy. During the 16th century the divided states of Italy proved vulnerable to invasions by unified kingdoms such as France and the Holy Roman Empire, which included Germany and the Netherlands.

THE CONQUEROR

In 1501 Michelangelo returned to Florence. Peace had been restored, and the new leader of the city council, Pietro Soderini, was a friend of the artist. Michelangelo's pietà had won him fame, and the governors of Florence Cathedral decided to commission a work by him. The result was one of Michelangelo's most beautiful sculptures.

In a yard near the cathedral in Florence was a huge marble block. It was nicknamed "The Giant" and had lain there throughout Michelangelo's youth. A sculptor had begun work on it years before but had botched the job and given up. It was 18 feet (5.5 m) tall, weighed tons, and was coveted by every sculptor in Florence. The block was awarded to Michelangelo.

The furrowed brow and anxious expression of Michelangelo's *David* suggest a hero gearing himself up mentally for the battle with Goliath. Scaffolding allowed the artist to reach all parts of the block and carve a figure three times lifesize.

SYMBOL OF FLORENCE

The young artist decided to carve a statue of David from the block. David was a king from the Old Testament, who in his youth had killed a giant, Goliath, stunning him with a stone from his sling and cutting off his head. Florentines saw this hero as a symbol for their own city-state, small but independent. Several other statues of David had been produced by Florentine artists, including Verrocchio. The Cathedral governors guaranteed the artist two years' salary, and in September 1501 he set to work with hammer and chisel.

Verrocchio's statue, 1473, shows David as a boy with Goliath's head at his feet.

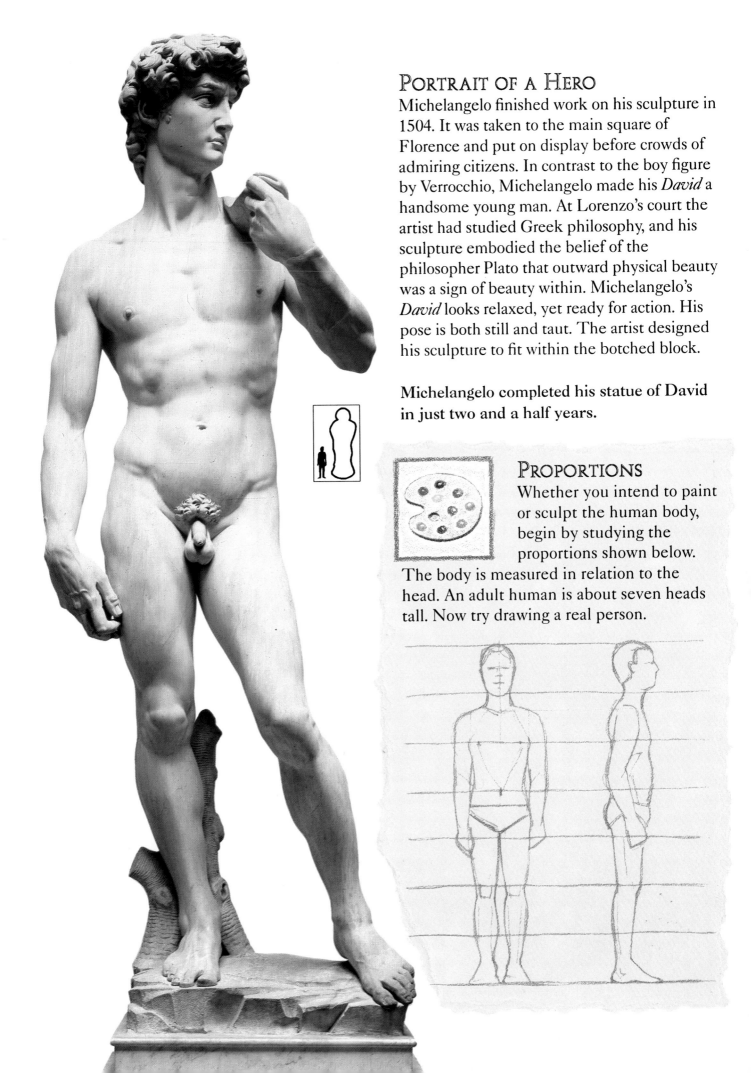

PORTRAIT OF A HERO

Michelangelo finished work on his sculpture in 1504. It was taken to the main square of Florence and put on display before crowds of admiring citizens. In contrast to the boy figure by Verrocchio, Michelangelo made his *David* a handsome young man. At Lorenzo's court the artist had studied Greek philosophy, and his sculpture embodied the belief of the philosopher Plato that outward physical beauty was a sign of beauty within. Michelangelo's *David* looks relaxed, yet ready for action. His pose is both still and taut. The artist designed his sculpture to fit within the botched block.

Michelangelo completed his statue of David in just two and a half years.

PROPORTIONS

Whether you intend to paint or sculpt the human body, begin by studying the proportions shown below. The body is measured in relation to the head. An adult human is about seven heads tall. Now try drawing a real person.

SCULPTOR AT WORK

Michelangelo's triumph in carving "David" was all the more remarkable because he had produced a number of other beautiful works during the same period. He also began a series of carvings that he never completed. These unfinished works tell us a great deal about how the artist set about creating his sculptures.

IN DEMAND

The years 1501-05 were busy. Michelangelo carved a marble sculpture of the Virgin and Child for a merchant from Bruges, and made a *David* in bronze for a French nobleman. Commissions came quickly and frequently. For his part, the artist seems to have found it hard to turn down offers and took on more than he could accomplish. He promised 15 statues for Siena Cathedral, but produced only two. He agreed to carve sculptures of the 12 apostles for Florence Cathedral, but began work on only one, St. Matthew. This habit of taking on too much work was to prove a source of anxiety throughout his career.

This unfinished sculpture shows that Michelangelo's method was to work from the front and carve backwards, rather than working on the figure from all sides, which is usual. The knee that juts out at the front is nearly finished, but in the center of the block the head has only just begun to emerge.

Michelangelo began *St. Matthew* in 1503, but it was never completed.

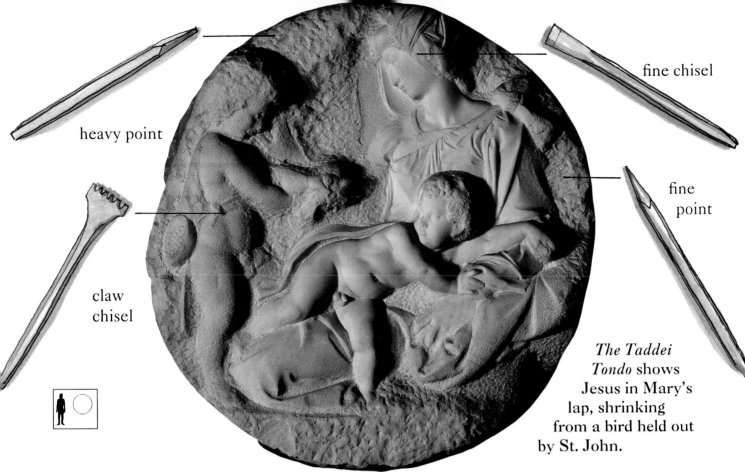

heavy point

claw chisel

fine chisel

fine point

The Taddei Tondo shows Jesus in Mary's lap, shrinking from a bird held out by St. John.

CARVING IN PROGRESS

At this time Michelangelo also began a *tondo*, or round work, in relief. The work was never finished, but you can see the marks of all the different tools used for carving, which sculptors still use today. First the stone was roughly hacked away with a heavy- and then a fine-pointed chisel. You can see lines left by these tools. The forms of the figures were developed with a claw, and then fine chisels were used to carve delicate details. Finally the work was smoothed and then polished by rubbing it with abrasives. All of this was dusty, strenuous work that required strength and stamina as well as great skill.

CARVING IN RELIEF

Try relief carving with a block of wax or soap, and linocutting or modeling tools. Mark your design on the block with a felt-tip pen. Place your block on newspaper and steady it with your gloved hand. Make a groove around the outline with a v-shaped tool (1). Pare away the background with a flatter tool (2). Using the same tool, round the edges (3). Smooth off any rough parts and put in details with a fine tool (4).

1 2 3 4

RIVAL ARTISTS

In 1504 the Signoria, the ruling council of Florence, commissioned Michelangelo to paint a mural (wall painting) for the council palace. It was to represent the battle of Cascina, in which Florence had triumphed over the neighboring city of Pisa. The project brought Michelangelo into rivalry with another Florentine artist, Leonardo da Vinci.

TRIAL OF SKILL

Leonardo da Vinci (1452-1519) was famed throughout Europe. The Signoria had commissioned him to depict the battle of Anghiari, between Florence and Milan, in the same room as Michelangelo's mural. It was seen as a contest between the two artists who disliked one another and were very different in character. In his 50s, Leonardo was charming and courteous. At 29, Michelangelo was blunt and awkward, and could be short-tempered.

Study for *The Battle of Cascina*, 1504

Leonardo da Vinci's drawing of the Virgin and Child, St. Anne and St. John (1500).

In the end, neither artist completed his task. Leonardo used experimental paints that did not work. Michelangelo produced a cartoon, or full-sized drawing, and figure studies, but before he could complete the project he was summoned to Rome by Pope Julius II.

A Wedding Gift

Around 1503 a Florentine lord named Agnolo Doni asked Michelangelo to paint a picture to celebrate his marriage. Like the carved *tondo*, the painting is circular, and it shows the Holy Family: Jesus, Mary, and her husband Joseph. The organization or composition of this work, with its tightly knit figures, was influenced by the work of Leonardo da Vinci, whose drawings and paintings of groups of figures interacting with one another (see opposite page) were much admired.

The *Doni Tondo* was painted between 1503-05.

In the background of the *Doni Tondo* the artist painted a group of male nudes, representing the classical age before Christianity. The boy in the mid-ground is St. John the Baptist, who announced the coming of Jesus.

The *Doni Tondo* was painted in tempera, using pigments (colors) mixed with egg yolk. Tempera colors dry quickly to give a glossy, brilliant effect. Michelangelo defined his foreground figures so sharply they look as if they were carved from a single block of stone. This technique separates the Holy Family from the mistier figures and landscape behind them.

Composition

Like the drawing by Leonardo (opposite), the *Doni Tondo* is based on the shape of the triangle. Mary's legs form the base of a large triangle, with Jesus at its tip. A smaller triangle links the three heads. Base a composition of your own on simple shapes. Experiment with your shapes in different positions until you reach the arrangement you find most pleasing.

PAPAL GLORY

Julius II had been elected pope in 1503. He was not only head of the Christian Church but ruler of a large state. In the fourteenth century the papacy had become weakened, and some wealth and territory had been lost. Julius was determined to restore its former glory, with the help of great artists like Michelangelo.

IN THE SERVICE OF THE POPE

In answer to the pope's summons, Michelangelo arrived in Rome in 1505. Julius planned to rebuild the Vatican, his palace in Rome, and the great church of St. Peter's, and charged Michelangelo to sculpt a tomb for him there. The artist spent months at the quarries of Carrara (above) selecting blocks of the finest snow-white marble. But when he returned to Rome, the pope refused either to pay for marble or see him. Dismayed, Michelangelo returned to Florence. But in 1506 he was reconciled with Julius and was commissioned to make a giant bronze sculpture of him for Bologna Cathedral.

The nine central panels of the Sistine Ceiling depict God's creation of heaven and earth, the temptation and fall of the first man and woman, Adam and Eve (above), and the story of Noah and the flood.

After finishing the bronze of Julius, the artist expected to begin work on the tomb. But the pope charged him instead to paint the ceiling of the Sistine Chapel in the Vatican. Michelangelo complained that he was a sculptor, not a painter. The project itself was very daunting. The ceiling was to be painted in fresco, a technique Michelangelo had not used since his apprenticeship in Florence. But Julius was adamant that he should carry out the work.

PLANNING THE SISTINE CEILING

Julius's plan for the ceiling was to have pictures of the 12 apostles painted in the triangular panels that linked walls and ceiling. The huge central area was to be decorated only with a pattern of geometric shapes. Despite his early reluctance to take on the project, Michelangelo made a far more ambitious suggestion. He proposed to use the central area to illustrate the history of the Old Testament from the Creation to Noah. He would include seven biblical prophets and five sibyls, female prophets from classical myth. The pope approved this, and Michelangelo set to work.

The Delphic Sibyl is one of five female prophets painted on the Sistine Ceiling.

FORESHORTENING

On the Sistine Ceiling Michelangelo painted the human body in every possible position, using the techniques of perspective and foreshortening. *Perspective* makes parts of the body appear large or small, depending on how close they are to the viewer. Limbs may also look shorter, or be entirely hidden, if they are pointing directly at the viewer; this is *foreshortening*. You can see how this works here: notice how the upper legs seem to disappear when a person is sitting down. Practice drawing a seated model yourself, then study and draw your model in kneeling and crouching positions.

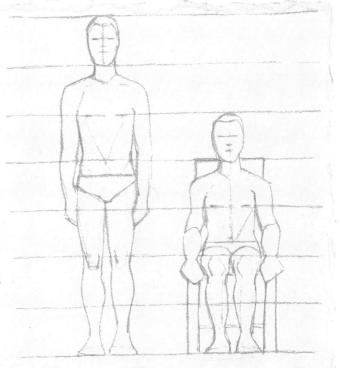

MIRACULOUS CEILING

The painting of the Sistine Ceiling began in 1508. Michelangelo was determined to carry out the work alone, instead of using assistants as was usual, particularly for large-scale projects. He completed the ceiling in four years, one of the greatest achievements in the history of art.

A DANGEROUS JOB

Michelangelo painted the Sistine Ceiling using the traditional fresco technique (see opposite page). It was an extremely difficult, even dangerous task. The area of the ceiling was 5,600 square feet (520 square m), the size of a tennis court. It curved down like a barrel to meet the walls. Perched on scaffolding 50 feet (16 m) above the floor of the chapel, Michelangelo had to bend over backwards and paint above his head. Drops of paint splattered his face all day long, and by evening his body was so cramped that he could only read letters from his family by holding them above his head.

Michelangelo drew this study in red chalk for *The Creation of Adam*.

Detail from the Sistine Ceiling, showing God creating heaven and earth.

STORMY RELATIONS

Michelangelo's relationship with the pope remained tempestuous. Julius II was a member of the powerful della Rovere family. His uncle had been pope before him. He was a man of great energy and ambition, a warrior who personally led his armies in battle. He was impatient with those who worked for him. He often visited the Sistine Chapel, climbing the scaffolding to see how work was progressing. He constantly asked Michelangelo how soon he could complete the project. Once, when the artist failed to give a satisfactory reply, he struck him with his staff, and on another occasion threatened to have him thrown from the scaffolding.

Despite these difficulties, Michelangelo's confidence and speed increased. His figures grew huge in scale, more muscular and energetic. At last, in October 1512 the ceiling was finished. The scaffolding was taken down and the citizens of Rome came to gaze at this breathtaking achievement. The whole ceiling was a celebration of human beauty and God's love for mankind, for the artist had covered it with hundreds of figures. At 37, he had proved himself a great painter as well as sculptor.

The Creation of Adam is one of the finest panels of the ceiling. It shows the moment of Adam's creation, as God's outstretched finger gives life to the first man. Eve, the first woman, shelters under God's arm.

FRESCO PAINTING

The word *fresco* means "fresh" in Italian. The artist applies paint to the surface of a freshly plastered wall. As the plaster dries, the paint bonds with it, to become part of the wall. Each day the artist must work quickly to finish the area of wet plaster. He must prepare carefully. Michelangelo pinned full-sized cartoon drawings to the plaster, and pressed along the outlines with a pointed tool so that he could follow the grooves in the plaster when the drawing was removed.

THE TRAGEDY OF THE TOMB

By 1512 Michelangelo was at the height of his powers. Yet the triumph of the Sistine Ceiling was followed by a period of frustration and unfinished projects. Of these, the most notorious was the tomb of Julius II. What Michelangelo later called "the tragedy of the tomb" was to dog the artist for the next 33 years.

DEATH OF JULIUS

With the completion of the Sistine Ceiling, Michelangelo returned to the tomb of Julius II. The task became more urgent when Julius died in 1513, and the contract was renewed with his heirs. The new pope, Leo X, was Giovanni de' Medici, whom Michelangelo had known as a boy in the Medici Palace. At first Leo was content to allow the artist to work on the tomb. By 1516 he had carved the awesome statue of Moses, one of six twice-lifesize figures planned for the upper tier of the tomb, and two smaller statues of slaves.

Michelangelo carved *Moses* between 1513-16.

Julius II, Michelangelo's greatest patron, painted by the artist Raphael (1483-1520)

PORTRAIT OF A PROPHET

Moses was the leader of the Israelites from the Old Testament. He received God's ten commandments on tablets of stone. Michelangelo sculpted the prophet clutching the tablets with bulging muscles. His tense pose and fierce expression suggest frustrated energy. You may notice the pair of horns on Moses' head. These were due to a mistranslation of the Hebrew phrase for "beams of light," which the Bible described as radiating from the prophet's forehead.

The Dying Slave was one of 12 statues of slaves planned to symbolize the arts, crushed by the death of Pope Julius.

The original design for Julius's tomb was very ambitious, with plans for 40 statues by Michelangelo. But in 1516 the sculptor went to work for the Medici in Florence. He worked on the project when he could, but it was not finished for 30 years. Later contracts bound him to produce fewer and fewer sculptures. The final contract was fulfilled when the artist delivered Moses and two female prophets, Rachel and Leah. The saga ended in 1545, when the artist was 70.

CLASSICAL SCULPTURE

In Renaissance times there was great excitement when ancient sculptures were unearthed in the ruins of Rome. In 1506 Michelangelo was present when one of the greatest finds of all was discovered. This was the statue of the Trojan priest Laocoön, below. It shows Laocoön and his sons being attacked by sea snakes. Because of their writhing, twisting bodies, such sculptures are known as *figura serpentinata*. They inspired Michelangelo's carvings, including *The Dying Slave*, left.

WORKING FOR THE MEDICI

In 1516 Michelangelo went back to Florence to work for the Medici family, who had returned to power there in 1512 with the help of Giovanni de' Medici, Pope Leo X. The sculptor spent much of the next 18 years in the service of the powerful family that had championed and supported him as a boy.

THE MEDICI CHAPEL

To celebrate the revived fortunes of his family, Leo planned to rebuild the Medici church of San Lorenzo in Florence. Michelangelo was appointed to design the chapel and carve monuments for the tombs of four of the Medici: Lorenzo the Magnificent, his brother Giuliano, and two dukes, also called Lorenzo and Giuliano, captains in the pope's army who had died young. It was another tremendous undertaking. Michelangelo worked on the project until 1534, but only completed statues of the two young dukes, presiding over symbolic figures.

Marble for the tombs was taken from the finest quarries in Italy, at Carrara, northwest of Florence. Carrara provided stone for the sculptors of ancient Rome, for Renaissance craftsmen. The quarries are still in use today. Michelangelo selected only the whitest marble amongst seams of rock streaked with gray and purple markings.

Statues of river gods were planned for the base of the tombs, but never carved.

Duke Giuliano, in Roman armour, watches over figures representing Night and Day.

The message of the tombs seems to be that with the passing of time, indicated by the symbolic figures, the glory even of Medici princes must end. The Medici remained in power in both Rome and Florence for most of the period 1516-34. When Pope Leo died in 1521 he was soon succeeded by his cousin Giulio, also a friend of Michelangelo from Lorenzo's palace.

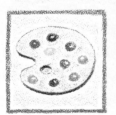

Lost in thought, Duke Lorenzo sits above the statues of Dawn and Dusk.

Like the other sculptures, the figure of Dawn looks very sorrowful. She seems dejected rather than hopeful at the prospect of the new day she announces.

The tombs of Michelangelo's first patron, Lorenzo the Magnificent, and his brother Giuliano were never completed. Their remains lie to this day in a simple chest by the altar in San Lorenzo.

PLANNING A SCULPTURE

When carving in the round, plan your work first. Keep your design simple and solid, or parts may flake off as you carve. Sketches can help with parts you find complicated. Keep in mind the dimensions of your block. Finally, make lifesize drawings from front and side. Transfer the drawings onto the block with a felt-tip pen, and redraw your marks as you carve them away.

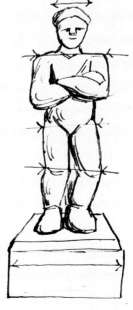

FLORENCE IN TURMOIL

Between 1527 and 1530, Medici control of Florence was interrupted. The city expelled its rulers and declared itself a republic. Despite his close relations with the Medici, Michelangelo found himself a prominent citizen of the republic. He was appointed architect in charge of the fortifications of the city.

In Renaissance times it was not so unusual for an artist to be employed as an architect or even as a military adviser. Michelangelo's old rival, Leonardo da Vinci, had designed many ingenious new weapons. Michelangelo, too, excelled as an architect as well as painter and sculptor. His design for the library for the church of San Lorenzo (above) had been revolutionary. He was also renowned as a poet!

IMPRISONED IN STONE

The della Rovere family continued to press Michelangelo to complete the tomb of Julius II. To placate them, the sculptor began five more statues of slaves. These are examples of *figura serpentinata*, showing the human form in twisting, violent movement. In their various stages of completeness, they seem to struggle to escape from the marble that encases them. A poem by Michelangelo expresses his belief that the sculptor's task was to free the shape already imprisoned in the stone, a process of discovery rather than creation.

Michelangelo carved this statue of Victory during the period of Florence's independence from Medici rule.

Below: *Bearded Slave*

Chisel marks can still be seen on the face of the Virgin Mary. Some people feel that the carvings Michelangelo left unfinished and rough are even more beautiful than his highly polished works. Do you agree?

Virgin and Child, carved for the altar of the Medici Chapel between 1524-34.

THE MEDICI RESTORED

The new republic did not last long. In 1529 the city was surrounded by armies allied to the new Medici pope, Clement VII. Michelangelo's fortifications held up well, but the city's resistance was worn away by a winter siege, and in 1530 the pope's armies entered the city. Frightened of punishment for his support of the republic, Michelangelo went into hiding, but Clement sent word he would be pardoned if he continued with the Medici tombs. The sculptor emerged and set to work again.

CARVING IN 3D

Make this carving in wax or soap with the tools listed on page 13. Work on newspaper and steady your carving with a gloved hand. Always carve away from your hand and body. Using a large, flattish tool, work from the front to pare away excess material almost as far as the outline marked. Do the same from the side. Now work from all sides to round off your sculpture and slowly reveal the form. Keep the block solid for as long as possible. Put in details with a fine tool.

THE LAST JUDGMENT

When Florence fell to Pope Clement VII in 1530, a new Medici was installed to rule the city. Alessandro de' Medici was a tyrant who hated Michelangelo, and only the pope's support protected him in Florence. In 1534 the artist's father died. Michelangelo left for the safety of Rome and never returned to his native city.

Detail from *The Last Judgment*; the souls of the damned are dragged to Hell.

In September 1534 Pope Clement died. The new pope, Paul III, was another great patron. He was eager to employ Michelangelo, declaring that he had waited 30 years to have him in his service! The project was a new fresco for the Sistine Chapel, this time for the great wall behind the altar. It was another huge task, since the wall was 45 by 40 feet (14 x 12 m), the largest ever faced by an artist. The subject was the Last Judgment, when human souls will rise from the dead to be judged by Christ and sent to Heaven or Hell. Michelangelo planned a great circling composition to portray this theme.

PAINTING HUMAN BEAUTY

In 1535 Michelangelo began work in the chapel whose ceiling he had finished 23 years before. Here, as so often before, his first aim was to show the beauty of the human body. But the mood in Rome had become more conservative. One of the pope's officials, Biagio da Cesena, objected to the nudity in the fresco, and in revenge, the artist painted his portrait as Minos, King of Hell, clothed only in the coils of a serpent.

Detail: flanked by his mother, Mary, Christ damns the wicked souls to Hell.

The story of *The Last Judgment* begins at the bottom left corner of the painting. The souls of the dead rise from their graves at the sound of the angels' trumpets. Angels help the souls ascend to meet Christ, shown with his mother, Mary, in the center. He is surrounded by saints, who carry symbols of their martyrdom.

The Last Judgment, 1535-41

Christ's hand is raised to damn the wicked souls to Hell. On the right of the painting the despairing figures of the damned are dragged down by grinning demons. They are ferried to Hell by Charon, a figure from Greek mythology, who strikes them with the oar from his boat. You can see Biagio da Cesena as King Minos in the bottom right corner.

Michelangelo painted *The Last Judgment* in his mid-60s. He worked more slowly, still without help from his assistants. He survived a fall from the scaffolding to finish the wall in 1541. People came to marvel at its beauty and were terrified by Michelangelo's vision of the end of the world.

When Pope Paul III first saw the painting, he fell on his knees, begging God not to punish him for his sins. In the end, however, Biagio da Cesena's criticism prevailed, and in 1564 one of Michelangelo's assistants, Daniele da Volterra, was appointed to paint draperies on the naked figures.

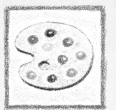

ROVING EYES

Michelangelo planned *The Last Judgment* so that our eyes move clockwise to follow the story from the bottom left corner upwards, across and down to the bottom right corner. You too can plan an interesting journey for eyes looking at your work. One of the ways to do this is in a strip cartoon. Strip cartoons are usually read from left to right along a line, like written words, but you can create interest by altering the size and shape of your cartoon boxes, or by leaving some pictures unframed.

FINAL YEARS

Michelangelo finished "The Last Judgment" at the age of 66. In Renaissance times people were fortunate to reach this age, yet Michelangelo lived on for another 23 years. He had never married. In his old age he worked mainly as an architect, although he also produced fine paintings and sculptures.

PETER AND PAUL

Delighted with *The Last Judgment*, in 1542 the pope commissioned Michelangelo to paint two large frescoes in the chapel of St. Paul in the Vatican. The subjects were the crucifixion of St. Peter and the conversion of St. Paul to Christianity. Now in his late 60s, Michelangelo found fresco painting tiring. As usual, he had to work in cramped conditions perched on rickety scaffolding, and there was always the race against time to complete the area of wet plaster. He finished both frescoes by 1550. During this time he also carved the statues of Rachel and Leah for the tomb of Julius II. The tomb was unveiled in 1547, more than 40 years after the project had been first proposed.

Conversion of St. Paul, 1542-45

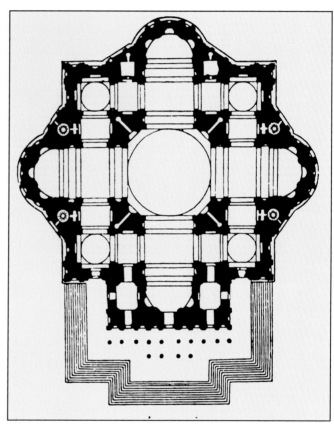

Ground plan of the dome of St. Peter's

Michelangelo's fresco shows the conversion of St. Paul when riding to the city of Damascus. Paul had persecuted Christians until he was struck down by a light from God. As Michelangelo grew older, so the bodies he carved and painted grew more massive and heavily muscled, as if they reflected his own aging body. He portrayed Paul as an old man, despite the fact that in the Bible his conversion happened when he was young.

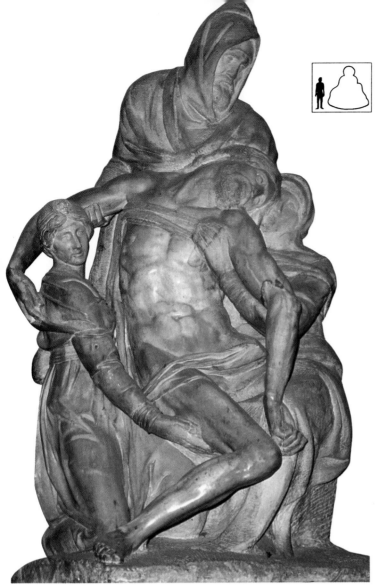

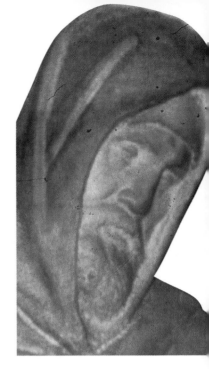

Even in old age, Michelangelo's passion for sculpture continued. This carving includes the artist's self-portrait as Nicodemus (right). You can see Michelangelo's misshapen nose, broken many years before in a fight with a fellow apprentice in Lorenzo's court.

This sculpture shows Christ being carried to his tomb. It was carved between 1547-55.

In his 70s and 80s, Michelangelo kept working, mainly as an architect, planning rather than carving in stone. He designed a beautiful square in Rome and the great dome of St. Peter's. He outlived Paul III and three more popes, working without pay to supervise the building of St. Peter's. Dedicated and solitary, in the last week of his life he was carving a pietà. He died in 1564, at the age of 89. He was honored in Rome as a great artist, then buried in Florence.

DESIGNING A HOME

Michelangelo's architecture was both beautiful and functional. Try your hand at architecture by designing your ideal house. Think of all the activities you enjoy and design spaces where they can take place. Rooms can be rectangular, round, or any shape you want. If you want an art room for painting and sculpture, you should plan large windows to let in light; a darkroom for photography could be small and windowless. You might plan a spiral staircase, a large recreational area, or a tower to use as an observatory.

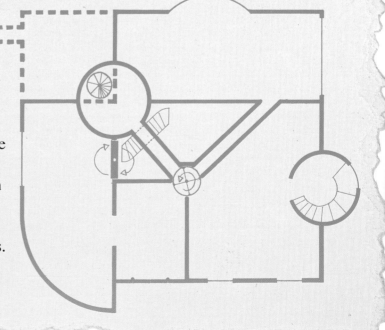

CHRONOLOGY OF MICHELANGELO'S LIFE

1475 Born in Caprese, near Florence.

1488 Apprenticed to the painter Ghirlandaio.

1489 Studied sculpture in the palace of Lorenzo de' Medici.

1492 Death of Lorenzo.

1494-95 Traveled to Venice and Bologna in search of commissions.

1496-1501 In Rome. Carved *Bacchus* and *The Pietà*.

1501-05 In Florence. Carved *David* and undertook various other commissions.

1505 Traveled to Rome to work for Pope Julius II.

1506-08 Made bronze statue of Julius II for Bologna Cathedral.

1508-12 Painted the ceiling of the Sistine Chapel in the Vatican in Rome.

1513-16 Began work on the tomb of Julius II.

1516-34 In Florence, working for the Medici.

1519-34 Carved statues for the Medici Chapel.

1527-30 Florence declared a republic.

1530 Florence invaded; Michelangelo spent several months in hiding.

1534 Settled in Rome.

1535-41 Painted *The Last Judgment*.

1538 Designed the piazza for the Capitoline Hill in Rome.

1542-45 Painted *The Conversion of St. Paul.*

1545 The tomb of Julius II finally completed.

1546-50 Painted *The Crucifixion of St. Peter.*

1547 Appointed principal architect of St. Peter's in Rome.

1564 Died in Rome at the age of 89. Buried in Florence.

A BRIEF HISTORY OF ART

The world's earliest works of art are figurines dating from 30,000 B.C. Cave art developed from 16,000 B.C. In the Classical Age (500-400 B.C.) sculpture flourished in Ancient Greece.

The Renaissance period began in Italy in the 1300s and reached its height in the sixteenth century. Famous Italian artists include Giotto (ca. 1266-1337), Leonardo da Vinci (1452-1519), **Michelangelo Buonarroti** (1475-1564), and Titian (ca. 1487-1576).

In Europe during the fifteenth and sixteenth centuries, Hieronymus Bosch (active 1480-1516), Albrecht Dürer (1471-1528), Pieter Breughel the Elder (1525-69), and El Greco (1541-1614) produced great art. Artists of the Baroque period include Peter Paul Rubens (1577-1640) and Rembrandt van Rijn (1606-69).

During the Romantic movement, English artists J.M.W. Turner (1775-1851) and John Constable (1776-1837) produced wonderful landscapes. Francisco Goya (1746-1828) was a great Spanish portrait artist.

Impressionism began in France in the 1870s. Artists include Claude Monet (1840-1926), Camille Pissarro (1830-1903), and Edgar Degas (1834-1917). Post-impressionists include Paul Cézanne (1839-1906), Paul Gauguin (1848-1903), and Vincent van Gogh (1853-90).

The twentieth century has seen many movements in art. Georges Braque (1882-1963) painted in the Cubist tradition, Salvador Dali (1904-89) in the Surrealist. Pablo Picasso (1881-1973) was a prolific Spanish painter. More recently Jackson Pollock (1912-56) and David Hockney (1937-) have achieved fame.

MUSEUMS AND GALLERIES

The museums, churches, and galleries listed below have examples of Michelangelo's work:

Casa Buonarroti, Florence, Italy

Galleria della Accademia, Florence

Uffizi Gallery, Florence

Church of San Lorenzo, Florence

Cathedral, Florence

Church of St. Peter's, Rome, Italy

The Vatican Palace, Rome

Church of Santa Maria sopra Minerva, Rome

Church of San Pietro in Vincoli, Rome

Museo dei Castello Sforzesco, Milan, Italy

Church of Notre Dame, Bruges, Belgium

The Louvre, Paris, France

Royal Academy, London, England

GLOSSARY

Cartoon A full-sized drawing made in preparation for a painting, particularly for a fresco. The cartoon was pinned to the wall to be painted. Prickmarks were usually made along the outlines of the drawing. The artist then dusted his cartoon with charcoal, so that when it was removed the marks of the outlines would be left on the wall.

Carving in the round A three-dimensional sculpture designed to be viewed from all sides.

Fresco The traditional method of making a wall painting, popular during the Renaissance. The word means "fresh" or "cold" in Italian. The artist applied paint directly onto the surface of a freshly plastered wall. As the paint dried it became part of the wall itself. Fresco colors were soft and muted. It was difficult for the fresco artist to correct his mistakes afterwards.

Pietà A painting or sculpture depicting the Virgin Mary cradling the body of her son, Jesus, after he had been crucified.

Pigments Colored powders mostly made from minerals from the earth, ground up and mixed with various binding substances to make paint of different kinds. For example, oil paints are pigments mixed with vegetable oil.

Relief A sculpture carved into a flat surface and designed to be seen from the front only.

Tempera A kind of paint made of pigment mixed with water and egg yolk. The colors are bright, and details painted in tempera are exact and clear.

Tondo A circular painting or sculpture.

INDEX

INDEX OF PICTURES

Special thanks to: The Bridgeman Art Library; The Trustees of the British Museum, London; Graphische Sammlung, Munich; Roger Vlitos. The publishers have made every effort to contact all the relevant copyright holders, and apologize for any omissions that may have inadvertently been made.